JAZZ PLAY ALONG

k and CD for B♭, E♭ and C Instruments

Produced by Mark Taylor

Arranged by Mark Taylor
and Jim Roberts

Disney

10 DISNEY CLASSICS

BOOK

CD

ISBN 978-0-634-05356-6

The following songs are the property of:
Bourne Company
Music Publishers
5 West 37th Street
New York, NY 10018

*Heigh Ho
Some Day My Prince Will Come
When You Wish Upon A Star
Whistle While You Work
Who's Afraid Of The Big Bad Wolf?*

Disney characters and artwork © Disney Enterprises, Inc.

HAL•LEONARD®
CORPORATION

7777 W. BLUEMOUND RD. P.O. BOX 13819 MILWAUKEE, WI 53213

Visit Hal Leonard Online at
www.halleonard.com

Disney

Produced by Mark Taylor
Arranged by Mark Taylor and Jim Roberts

Featured Players:

Graham Breedlove-Trumpet
John Desalme-Tenor Sax
Tony Nalker-Piano
Jim Roberts-Bass
Steve Fidyk-Drums

HOW TO USE THE CD:

Each song has <u>two</u> tracks:

1) Split Track/Melody

Woodwind, Brass, Keyboard, and Mallet Players can use this track as a learning tool for melody style and inflection.

Bass Players can learn and perform with this track – remove the recorded bass track by turning down the volume on the LEFT channel.

Keyboard and **Guitar Players** can learn and perform with this track – remove the recorded piano part by turning down the volume on the RIGHT channel.

2) Full Stereo Track

Soloists or **groups** can learn and perform with this accompaniment track with the RHYTHM SECTION only.

ALICE IN WONDERLAND
FROM WALT DISNEY'S ALICE IN WONDERLAND

WORDS BY BOB HILLIARD
MUSIC BY SAMMY FAIN

CD
1: SPLIT TRACK/MELODY
2: FULL STEREO TRACK

C VERSION

CRUELLA DE VIL
FROM WALT DISNEY'S ONE HUNDRED AND ONE DALMATIANS

WORDS AND MUSIC BY
MEL LEVEN

C VERSION

BEAUTY AND THE BEAST
FROM WALT DISNEY'S BEAUTY AND THE BEAST

C VERSION

LYRICS BY HOWARD ASHMAN
MUSIC BY ALAN MENKEN

HEIGH-HO

THE DWARF'S MARCHING SONG FROM DISNEY'S
SNOW WHITE AND THE SEVEN DWARFS

WORDS BY LARRY MOREY
MUSIC BY FRANK CHURCHILL

C VERSION

SOME DAY MY PRINCE WILL COME

FROM WALT DISNEY'S SNOW WHITE AND THE SEVEN DWARFS

WORDS BY LARRY MOREY
MUSIC BY FRANK CHURCHILL

WHEN YOU WISH UPON A STAR
FROM WALT DISNEY'S PINOCCHIO

WORDS BY NED WASHINGTON
MUSIC BY LEIGH HARLINE

C VERSION

WHISTLE WHILE YOU WORK
FROM WALT DISNEY'S SNOW WHITE AND THE SEVEN DWARFS

WORDS BY LARRY MOREY
MUSIC BY FRANK CHURCHILL

C VERSION

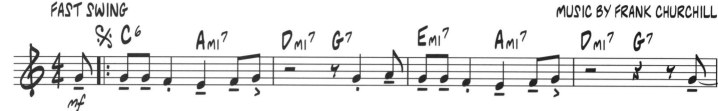

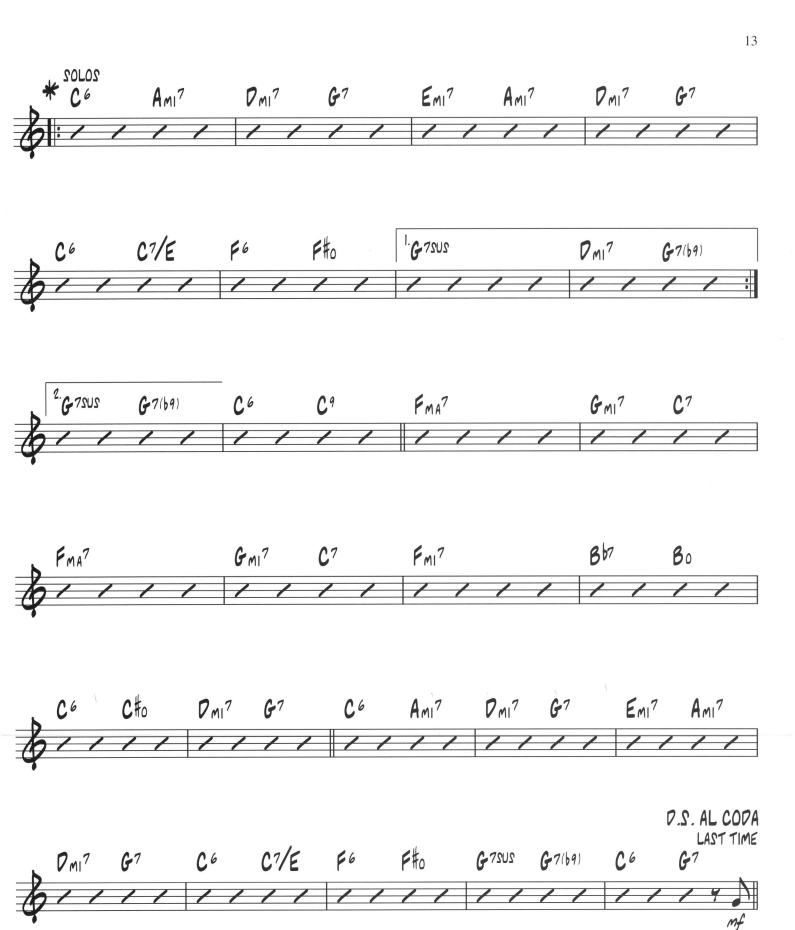

CD
15 : SPLIT TRACK/MELODY
16 : FULL STEREO TRACK

WHO'S AFRAID OF THE BIG BAD WOLF?

FROM WALT DISNEY'S THREE LITTLE PIGS

C VERSION

WORDS AND MUSIC BY FRANK CHURCHILL
ADDITIONAL LYRIC BY ANN RONELL

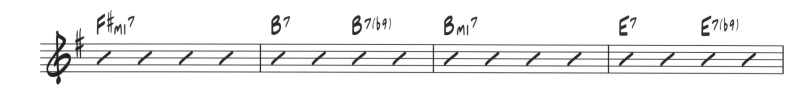

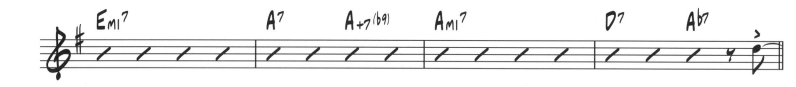

- **17** : SPLIT TRACK/MELODY
- **18** : FULL STEREO TRACK

YOU'VE GOT A FRIEND IN ME
FROM WALT DISNEY'S TOY STORY

C VERSION

MUSIC AND LYRICS BY
RANDY NEWMAN

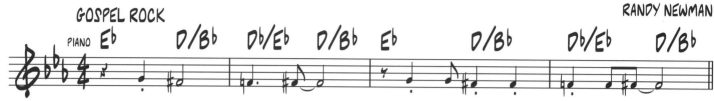

CD
19 : SPLIT TRACK/MELODY
20 : FULL STEREO TRACK

ZIP-A-DEE-DOO-DAH
FROM WALT DISNEY'S SONG OF THE SOUTH

WORDS BY RAY GILBERT
MUSIC BY ALLIE WRUBEL

C VERSION

19

CRUELLA DE VIL
FROM WALT DISNEY'S ONE HUNDRED AND ONE DALMATIANS

WORDS AND MUSIC BY
MEL LEVEN

B♭ VERSION

BEAUTY AND THE BEAST
FROM WALT DISNEY'S BEAUTY AND THE BEAST

Bb VERSION

LYRICS BY HOWARD ASHMAN
MUSIC BY ALAN MENKEN

HEIGH-HO
THE DWARF'S MARCHING SONG FROM DISNEY'S
SNOW WHITE AND THE SEVEN DWARFS

WORDS BY LARRY MOREY
MUSIC BY FRANK CHURCHILL

Bb VERSION

SOME DAY MY PRINCE WILL COME
FROM WALT DISNEY'S SNOW WHITE AND THE SEVEN DWARFS

CD
◆ 9 : SPLIT TRACK/MELODY
◆ 10 : FULL STEREO TRACK

Bb VERSION

WORDS BY LARRY MOREY
MUSIC BY FRANK CHURCHILL

WHEN YOU WISH UPON A STAR
FROM WALT DISNEY'S PINOCCHIO

WORDS BY NED WASHINGTON
MUSIC BY LEIGH HARLINE

Bb VERSION · SLOWLY

WHISTLE WHILE YOU WORK
FROM WALT DISNEY'S SNOW WHITE AND THE SEVEN DWARFS

WORDS BY LARRY MOREY
MUSIC BY FRANK CHURCHILL

Bb VERSION

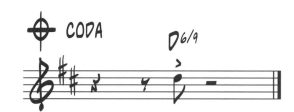

CD
15 : SPLIT TRACK/MELODY
16 : FULL STEREO TRACK

WHO'S AFRAID OF THE BIG BAD WOLF?
FROM WALT DISNEY'S THREE LITTLE PIGS

Bb VERSION

WORDS AND MUSIC BY FRANK CHURCHILL
ADDITIONAL LYRIC BY ANN RONELL

17: SPLIT TRACK/MELODY
18: FULL STEREO TRACK

YOU'VE GOT A FRIEND IN ME
FROM WALT DISNEY'S TOY STORY

MUSIC AND LYRICS BY
RANDY NEWMAN

Bb VERSION

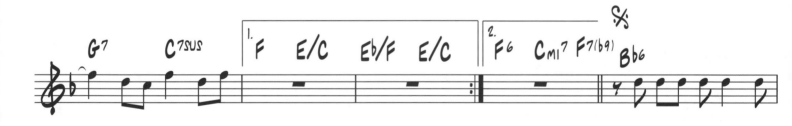

ZIP-A-DEE-DOO-DAH
FROM WALT DISNEY'S SONG OF THE SOUTH

WORDS BY RAY GILBERT
MUSIC BY ALLIE WRUBEL

Bb VERSION
FAST SWING

CD
1 : SPLIT TRACK/MELODY
2 : FULL STEREO TRACK

ALICE IN WONDERLAND
FROM WALT DISNEY'S ALICE IN WONDERLAND

WORDS BY BOB HILLIARD
MUSIC BY SAMMY FAIN

E♭ VERSION

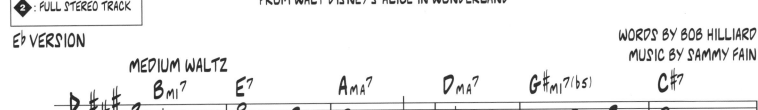

CRUELLA DE VIL
FROM WALT DISNEY'S ONE HUNDRED AND ONE DALMATIANS

WORDS AND MUSIC BY
MEL LEVEN

Eb VERSION

BEAUTY AND THE BEAST
FROM WALT DISNEY'S BEAUTY AND THE BEAST

Eb VERSION

LYRICS BY HOWARD ASHMAN
MUSIC BY ALAN MENKEN

HEIGH-HO
THE DWARF'S MARCHING SONG FROM DISNEY'S
SNOW WHITE AND THE SEVEN DWARFS

WORDS BY LARRY MOREY
MUSIC BY FRANK CHURCHILL

Eb VERSION

(BACK TO * FOR MORE SOLOS)

WHEN YOU WISH UPON A STAR
FROM WALT DISNEY'S PINOCCHIO

WORDS BY NED WASHINGTON
MUSIC BY LEIGH HARLINE

CD
⟨13⟩ : SPLIT TRACK/MELODY
⟨14⟩ : FULL STEREO TRACK

WHISTLE WHILE YOU WORK
FROM WALT DISNEY'S SNOW WHITE AND THE SEVEN DWARFS

Eb VERSION

WORDS BY LARRY MOREY
MUSIC BY FRANK CHURCHILL

FAST SWING

(BACK TO ✳ 2 MORE TIMES FOR SOLOS)

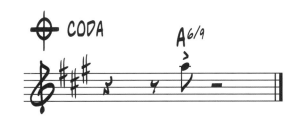

15 : SPLIT TRACK/MELODY
16 : FULL STEREO TRACK

WHO'S AFRAID OF THE BIG BAD WOLF?

FROM WALT DISNEY'S THREE LITTLE PIGS

Eb VERSION

WORDS AND MUSIC BY FRANK CHURCHILL
ADDITIONAL LYRIC BY ANN RONELL

YOU'VE GOT A FRIEND IN ME
FROM WALT DISNEY'S TOY STORY

Eb VERSION

MUSIC AND LYRICS BY
RANDY NEWMAN

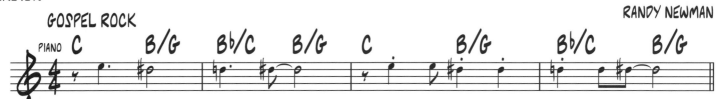

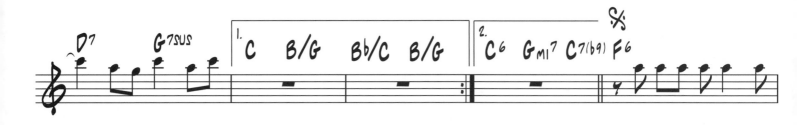

ZIP-A-DEE-DOO-DAH
FROM WALT DISNEY'S SONG OF THE SOUTH

WORDS BY RAY GILBERT
MUSIC BY ALLIE WRUBEL

Eb VERSION

ALICE IN WONDERLAND
FROM WALT DISNEY'S ALICE IN WONDERLAND

WORDS BY BOB HILLIARD
MUSIC BY SAMMY FAIN

CRUELLA DE VIL
FROM WALT DISNEY'S ONE HUNDRED AND ONE DALMATIANS

WORDS AND MUSIC BY
MEL LEVEN

BEAUTY AND THE BEAST

FROM WALT DISNEY'S BEAUTY AND THE BEAST

CD
- 5: SPLIT TRACK/MELODY
- 6: FULL STEREO TRACK

LYRICS BY HOWARD ASHMAN
MUSIC BY ALAN MENKEN

HEIGH-HO
THE DWARF'S MARCHING SONG FROM DISNEY'S
SNOW WHITE AND THE SEVEN DWARFS

WORDS BY LARRY MOREY
MUSIC BY FRANK CHURCHILL

Some Day My Prince Will Come
FROM WALT DISNEY'S SNOW WHITE AND THE SEVEN DWARFS

WORDS BY LARRY MOREY
MUSIC BY FRANK CHURCHILL

WHEN YOU WISH UPON A STAR
FROM WALT DISNEY'S PINOCCHIO

WORDS BY NED WASHINGTON
MUSIC BY LEIGH HARLINE

WHISTLE WHILE YOU WORK
FROM WALT DISNEY'S SNOW WHITE AND THE SEVEN DWARFS

WORDS BY LARRY MOREY
MUSIC BY FRANK CHURCHILL

(BACK TO ✳ 2 MORE TIMES FOR SOLOS)

CD
⬥ **15** : SPLIT TRACK/MELODY
⬥ **16** : FULL STEREO TRACK

WHO'S AFRAID OF THE BIG BAD WOLF?
FROM WALT DISNEY'S THREE LITTLE PIGS

WORDS AND MUSIC BY FRANK CHURCHILL
ADDITIONAL LYRIC BY ANN RONELL

♪: C VERSION

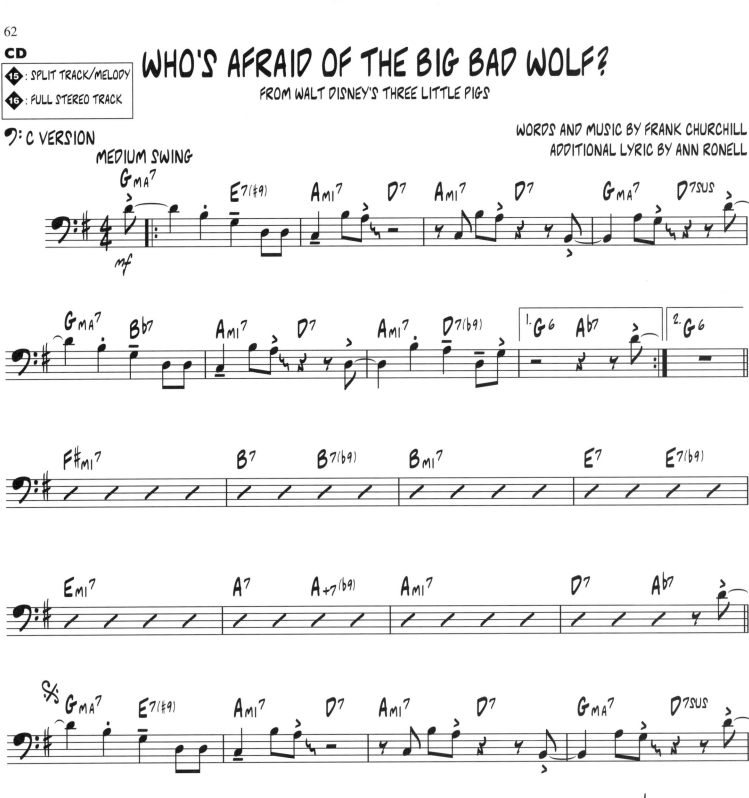

YOU'VE GOT A FRIEND IN ME
FROM WALT DISNEY'S TOY STORY

MUSIC AND LYRICS BY
RANDY NEWMAN

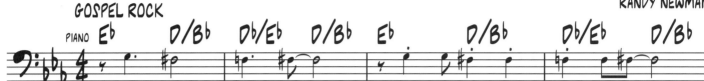

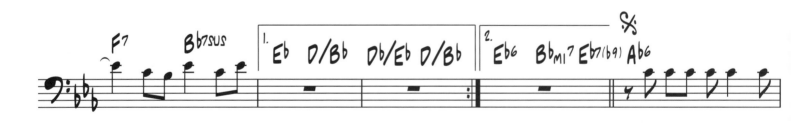

ZIP-A-DEE-DOO-DAH
FROM WALT DISNEY'S SONG OF THE SOUTH

WORDS BY RAY GILBERT
MUSIC BY ALLIE WRUBEL

Lyrics

ALICE IN WONDERLAND

Alice in Wonderland,
How do you get to Wonderland,
Over the hill or underland
Or just behind a tree?

When clouds go rolling by
They roll away and leave the sky.
Where is the land behind the eye
People cannot see?

Where can you see?
Where do the stars go?
Where is the crescent moon?
They must be somewhere
In the sunny afternoon.

Alice in Wonderland,
Where is the path to Wonderland,
Over the hill or here or there?
I wonder where.

BEAUTY AND THE BEAST

Tale as old as time, true as it can be.
Barely even friends, then somebody bends
Unexpectedly.

Just a little change.
Small, to say the least.
Both a little scared, neither one prepared.
Beauty and the Beast.

Ever just the same.
Ever a surprise.
Ever as before, ever just as sure
As the sun will rise.

Tale as old as time.
Tune as old as song.
Bittersweet and strange,
Finding you can change,
Learning you were wrong.

Certain as the sun rising in the East.
Tale as old as time, song as old as rhyme.
Beauty and the Beast.

Tale as old as time, song as old as rhyme
Beauty and the Beast.

CRUELLA DE VIL

Cruella De Vil, Cruella De Vil,
If she doesn't scare you
No evil thing will.
To see her is to take a sudden chill.
Cruella, Cruella De Vil.

The curl of her lips,
The ice in her stare;
All innocent children
Had better beware.
She's like a spider waiting for the kill.
Look out for Cruella De Vil.

At first you think Cruella is the devil,
But after time had worn away the shock,
You come to realize
You've seen her kind of eyes
Watching you from underneath a rock.

This vampire bat,
This inhuman beast,
She ought to be locked up
And never released.
The world was such a
Wholesome place until
Cruella, Cruella De Vil.

HEIGH-HO

"Heigh-ho, heigh-ho."
To make your troubles go,
Just keep on singing all day long,
"Heigh-ho, heigh-ho, heigh-ho."

"Heigh-ho, heigh-ho."
For if you're feeling low,
You positively can't go wrong with a
"Heigh, heigh-ho, heigh-ho."

"Heigh-ho, heigh-ho,"
It's home from work we go.
(whistle)
"Heigh-ho, heigh-ho, heigh-ho."

"Heigh-ho, heigh-ho,"
All seven in a row.
(whistle)
With a "Heigh, heigh-ho."

SOME DAY MY PRINCE WILL COME

Some day my prince will come,
Some day I'll find my love,
And how thrilling that moment will be,
When the prince of my dreams
Comes true to me.

He'll whisper "I love you"
And steal a kiss or two
Though he's far away
I'll find my love some day
Some day when my dreams come true.

Some day I'll find my love,
Some one to call my own,
And I'll know her the moment we meet,
For my heart will start skipping a beat.

Some day we'll say and do things
We've been longing to do
Though she's far away
I'll find my love some day
Some day when my dreams come true.

WHEN YOU WISH UPON A STAR

When you with upon a star,
Makes no diff'rence who you are.
Anything your heart desires
Will come to you.

If your heart is in your dream,
No request is too extreme.
When you wish upon a star
As dreamers do.

Fate is kind,
She brings to those who love,
The sweet fulfillment of
Their secret longing.

Like a bolt out of the blue,
Fate steps in and sees you thru.
When you wish upon a star
Your dream comes true.

WHISTLE WHILE YOU WORK

Just whistle while you work.
(whistle)
Put on that grin and start right in
To whistle loud and long.

Just hum a merry song.
(hum)
Just do your best then take a rest
And sing yourself a song.

When there's too much to do,
Don't let it bother you.
Forget your troubles, try to be
Just like a cheerful chick-a-dee.
And whistle while you work.
(whistle)
Come on, get smart,
Tune up and start
To whistle while you work.

WHO'S AFRAID OF THE BIG BAD WOLF?

Who's afraid of the big bad wolf,
Big bad wolf, big bad wolf?
Who's afraid of the big bad wolf?
Tra la la la la.

Who's afraid of the big bad wolf,
Big bad wolf, big bad wolf?
Who's afraid of the big bad wolf?
Tra la la la la.

ZIP-A-DEE-DOO-DAH

Zip-a-dee-doo-dah, zip-a-dee-ay.
My, oh my, what a wonderful day!
Plenty of sunshine, headin' my way.
Zip-a-dee-doo-dah, zip-a-dee-ay!

Mister Bluebird on my shoulder.
It's the truth, it's "actch'll."
Ev'rything is "satisfactch'll."

Zip-a-dee-doo-dah, zip-a-dee-ay!
Wonderful feeling, wonderful day.

YOU'VE GOT A FRIEND IN ME

You've got a friend in me.
You've got a friend in me.
When the road looks rough ahead,
And your miles and miles from your nice warm bed,
You just remember what your old pal said:
Son, you've got a friend in me.
Yeah, you've got a friend in me.

You've got a friend in me.
You've got a friend in me.
You got troubles, then I got 'em too.
There isn't anything I wouldn't do for you.
If we stick together we can see it through,
'Cause you've got a friend in me.
Yeah, you've got a friend in me.

Now, some other folks might be a little bit smarter than I am,
Bigger and stronger too.
Maybe. But none of them will ever love you the way I do,
Just me and you, boy.

And as the years go by,
Our friendship will never die.
You're gonna see it's our destiny.

You've got a friend in me.
You've got a friend in me.
You've got a friend in me.

JAZZ PLAY ALONG SERIES

BOOK/CD PACKAGES ONLY $14.95 EACH!

The JAZZ PLAY ALONG SERIES is the ultimate learning tool for all jazz musicians. With musician-friendly lead sheets, melody cues and other split track choices on the included CD, this first-of-its-kind package makes learning to play jazz easier than ever before.

FOR STUDY,
each tune includes a split track with:

■ Melody cue with proper style and inflection
■ Professional rhythm tracks
■ Choruses for soloing
■ Removable bass part
■ Removable piano part

FOR PERFORMANCE,
each tune also has:

■ An additional full stereo accompaniment track (no melody)
■ Additional choruses for soloing

DUKE ELLINGTON • Volume 1
Caravan • Don't Get Around Much Anymore • In a Mellow Tone • In a Sentimental Mood • It Don't Mean a Thing (If It Ain't Got That Swing) • Perdido • Prelude to a Kiss • Satin Doll • Sophisticated Lady • Take the "A" Train.
00841644

MILES DAVIS • Volume 2
All Blues • Blue in Green • Four • Half Nelson • Milestones • Nardis • Seven Steps to Heaven • So What • Solar • Tune Up.
00841645

THE BLUES • Volume 3
Billie's Bounce (Bill's Bounce) • Birk's Works • Blues for Alice • Blues in the Closet • C-Jam Blues • Freddie Freeloader • Mr. P.C. • Now's the Time • Tenor Madness • Things Ain't What They Used to Be.
00841646

JAZZ BALLADS • Volume 4
Body and Soul • But Beautiful • Here's That Rainy Day • Misty • My Foolish Heart • My Funny Valentine • My One and Only Love • My Romance • The Nearness of You • (includes lyric sheets).
00841691

THE BEST OF BEBOP • Volume 5
Anthropology • Donna Lee • Doxy • Epistrophy • Lady Bird • Oleo • Ornithology • Scrapple from the Apple • Woodyn' You • Yardbird Suite.
00841689

JAZZ CLASSICS WITH EASY CHANGES • Volume 6
Comin' Home Baby • Blue Train • Footprints • Impressions • Killler Joe • Moanin' • Sidewinder • St. Thomas • Stolen Moments • Well You Needn't (It's Over Now).
00841690

ESSENTIAL JAZZ STANDARDS Volume 7
Autumn Leaves • Cotton Tail • Easy Living • I Remember You • If I Should Lose You • Lullaby of Birdland • Out of Nowhere • Stella by Starlight • There Will Never Be Another You • When Sunny Gets Blue.
00843000

ANTONIO CARLOS JOBIM AND THE ART OF THE BOSSA NOVA Volume 8
The Girl From Ipanema (Garota De Ipanema) • How Insensitive (Insensatez) • Meditation (Meditacao) • Once I Loved (Amor Em Paz) (Love in Peace) • One Note Samba (Samba De Uma Nota So) • Quiet Nights of Quiet Stars (Corcovado) • Slightly out of Tune (Desafinado) • So Danco Samba (Jazz 'N' Samba) • Triste • Wave.
00843001

DIZZY GILLESPIE • Volume 9
Birk's Works • Con Alma • Groovin' High • Manteca • A Night in Tunisia • Salt Peanuts • Shawnuff • Things to Come • Tour De Force • Woodyn' You.
00843002

DISNEY CLASSICS • Volume 10
Alice in Wonderland • Beauty and the Beast • Cruella De Vil • Heigh-Ho • Some Day My Prince Will Come • When You Wish Upon a Star • Whistle While You Work • Who's Afraid of the Big Bad Wolf • You've Got a Friend in Me • Zip-a-Dee-Doo-Dah.
00843003

RODGERS AND HART • Volume 11
The Blue Room • Dancing on the Ceiling • Bewitched • Have You Met Miss Jones? • I Could Write a Book • The Lady Is a Tramp • Little Girl Blue • My Romance • There's a Small Hotel • You Are Too Beautiful.
00843004

ESSENTIAL JAZZ CLASSICS Volume 12
Airegin • Ceora • The Frim Fram Sauce • Israel • Milestones • Nefertiti • Red Clay • Satin Doll • Song for My Father • Take Five.
00843005

JOHN COLTRANE • Volume 13
Blue Train (Blue Trane) • Countdown • Cousin Mary • Equinox • Giant Steps • Impressions • Lazy Bird • Mr. P.C. • Moment's Notice • Naima (Neima).
00843006

IRVING BERLIN • Volume 14
Be Careful, It's My Heart • Blue Skies • Change Partners • Cheek to Cheek • How Deep Is the Ocean (How High Is the Sky) • I've Got My Love to Keep Me Warm • Let's Face the Music and Dance • Steppin' Out with My Baby • They Say It's Wonderful • What'll I Do?
00843007

RODGERS & HAMMERSTEIN Volume 15
Bali Ha'i • Do I Love You Because You're Beautiful? • Hello Young Lovers • I Have Dreamed • It Might As Well Be Spring • Love, Look Away • My Favorite Things • The Surrey with the Fringe on Top • The Sweetest Sounds • Younger Than Springtime.
00843008

COLE PORTER • Volume 16
All of You • At Long Last Love • Easy to Love (You'd Be So Easy to Love) • Ev'ry Time We Say Goodbye • I Concentrate on You • I've Got You Under My Skin • In the Still of the Night • It's All Right with Me • It's De-Lovely • You'd Be So Nice to Come Home To.
00843009

Prices, contents and availability subject to change without notice.

FOR MORE INFORMATION, SEE YOUR LOCAL MUSIC DEALER, OR WRITE TO:

HAL•LEONARD® CORPORATION
7777 W. BLUEMOUND RD. P.O. BOX 13819 MILWAUKEE, WI 53213

Visit Hal Leonard online at **www.halleonard.com**

0303